gwen
    & other poems

gwen
& other poems

by

Ann McGarrell

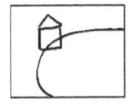

Cove House   New York

2012

Copyright © 2012 by Ann McGarrell
All rights reserved

Library of Congress Control Number: 2012934794

ISBN: 978-0-9833472-1-7

Gwen is based on the notes, letters, diaries, and paintings of the Welsh artist Gwen John (1876-1939).

Grateful acknowledge is made to the Musée Rodin for permission to reproduce *Self Portrait with Letter*, and to *Oyster Boy*, where "Mediterraneo" and "The Snow Cat" were first published.

Cover Art: Gwen John, "Self Portrait with Letter"
Pencil and watercolor on cream paper, 8 ¾ x 6 ¼ inches
Musée Rodin, Paris. Photo: Jean de Calan
Cover Design: Natsuko Kinoshita

Cove House Press
P. O. Box 1586
New York, NY 10013

for Sandra Bailey

My sister was amorous and proud.

– Augustus John

CONTENTS

GWEN

1904	Why, she is just like me	13
1905	Cher Monsieur Rodin	14
1905	In the rainy garden	15
1906	Screens scrims and jalousies	18
1906	I am more than a hole	19
1906	Love is my illness	20
1906	Why are you angry?	21
1907	I've brushed my hair a thousand	23
1907	Maître	24
1907	Will you come on Satyrday	25
1907	Aloneness is near God	26
1907	Arched in an arabesque	28
1908	This morning as you left	29
1908	I take the little train	30
1908	I am Miss Edgar-Quinet	32
1909	Your promises unkept	34
1910	There, almost at my feet	35
1912	I lay in bed all night	37
1914	The street trembles	38
1917	I was not there	39
1917	Rilke, help me	40
1919	They keep hay in it	41

1926   *Chère Mademoiselle Véra* . . . 42
1926   *Chère Mademoiselle* . . . 43
1930   *Delayed dismayed mislaid* . . . 44
1930   *I saw the Gate of Hell* . . . 46
1932   *Now all my things* . . . 48
1933   *Which region shall I wander* . . . 50
1936   *Blue shawl crumpled* . . . 51
1939   *Je vous salue Marie* . . . 52
1939   *The priest has come* . . . 54
1961   *:GUS   Fame and lust outlived by* . . . 56

MOVING OUT

Ten Japonaiseries . . . 61
VA   *Sun on the ridge* . . . 63

IN   *Dogwood and redbud* . . . 63
TX   *Rattlers, coyotes* . . . 64
NH   *Black ice* . . . 64
OR   *"A particularly subtle and delicate"* . . . 65
CA   *Lupines and poppies* . . . 65
PG   *Little towns that war* . . . 66
CH   *Don't believe what they say* . . . 67
VT   *The Snow Cat* . . . 68
AZ   *Nothing more different* . . . 70
NM   *"Eschewing the merely"* . . . 71

Mediterraneo . . . 72
From a Neutral Country . . . 74
Knossos . . . 76
The Puzzle Mistress . . . 78
Flo . . . 79
The Unfortunate Lady . . . 80

1904

>   (postcard from Bruges)

How is the cat?
>   *Dorelia*

Why, she is just like me,
frightened and fierce,
prowling the studio hour after hour.
At night she tucks her kitten in my box of silks
then comes to purr beside me
until dawn, patting my eyelids
when she wants her milk.

Léonard was here, all dour,
pierced to the very heart
but looking quite sportif.
Dodo, he is a haycart clod.
Gussy and Ida love you as he never could.

I miss you, *tu me manques beaucoup.*
I shall wear the grey dress
to a Certain Interview.

1905

Cher Monsieur Rodin,

I sought you all my life on country roads
but had I met you there
I would have run away.
Please excuse bad french,
my body and I will come to your atelier
at ten o'clock.

La muse de Whistler

1905

In the rainy garden
my straw hat collapsing
(shapeless, it will shape itself
to my head and dry)
my skirts heavy, draggled

I struggle up, push him
off with my wrists
all mud
                he kisses my loamy hand
(what can I do but laugh?)
                steps back, calls me his *hamadryade*,
a minor nymph, still draped
in thin wet russet wool.

Too banal to fall in love with the maître
but there it is, I have.

Ô mon roi soleil, dieu solaire,
fill me with fire and light
I am your chariot
I bear you down the day
no damp dryad –
can't you tell?

seeing touching smelling
me? The sun licks like a cat,
turns me taut and tawny, bold.
              Pumped out now, hitched up,
you scold me: *C'est fatigant, Je suis vieux,
moi.*
But not to me! I cry.
We walk to the station,
my beautiful empty room with a cat in it
beckons:
              à demain alors
You leave for Madame votre femme.
Some say she's not.
Now *there's* one you found in a hollow log
maître,
scary old clothespin mouth,
huge satin frock at noon –
sorry, sorry, je m'excuse, love,
mon amour unique – I mean: cher maître.
But – can't you pension her off?
That American countess, too.
And the rest, troupe of dazed daisies,
all padding starkers in the studio.
              Oui, j'aime bien les anglaises,
                elles ont des belles jambes longues.
The better to grip you with, my galaxy,

cradle you, my continent.
And Gussy says you called me *bel artiste.*
To me you said *Ne me quitte pas avant que ceci soit terminé*
touching me there, cupping the hollow of my thigh.
Keep it, do,
for as long as it takes.
Please keep it forever.

1906

Screens scrims and jalousies, yes,
but even in the dark armoire our heat this flame
must blaze all through the atelier
and people tramping in while we

you know

& then I tremble, filled with fear and rage
& bend down to fasten my stockings,
sit up, buttoning my bodice with rigid hands,
hearing your voice go calmly on
as if it were teatime at the vicar's.

Before I loved you, all my fires were banked.
Now I know what embers feel at night,
under dead ashes,
their brightness shut away, denied.

Tomorrow, if you are tired, we will only kiss.

1906

I am more than a hole
with some hair.

Remember that.

To memorize Euripides for you
is my dearest wish
for then I could be with you
while you work
and not be shy
oh when I spoke
it would be a great poet's eternal words
immortal as the children
we make together you and I
children of marble
and of bronze
fearless in their beauty.

1906

Love is my illness
you are my remedy

this is a drawing of my dear cat Edgar-Quinet
qui vous allez connaître très bientôt j'espère.
You will admire her stubborn character:
I sang *Sweet Alice* and then she bit my chin;
clearly she disapproves of thwarted love.

I waited in my room

you did not come.

1906

Why are you angry?
Of course I must stay in the woods
till I find Edgar.
Please don't worry
please don't imagine I shame you
in any way
those men who make stupid remarks about
pussy
are cowards and give up quickly
having displayed their brilliant wit
and dull appendages

      my body is turning a lovely biscuit color
                              in the sun
I smell deliciously of leaves and grass
& I won't get thin, I promise

I will not be pretty and happy for you without my cat

If you despise me now
all is finished for me
I will clean my room and die.

She came back this morning to the glade
making her little cross cry!
I breathed on her chilled paws.
The woman in the farmhouse gave us milk.

1907

I've brushed my hair a thousand strokes
it has a little gleam
and smells of honeysuckle
(why do they call it *chêvre-feuille, goat-leaf?*
please explain)
Edgar has a rose-coloured ribbon
    violets on the mantelpiece
        sun spills on my white chair

we wait for your soft pounce.

The stair gives one sharp cry.

1907

Maître,

It's kind of you to mourn for Ida.
I will tell my brother Augustus
(lui aussi il s'appelle 'Auguste').
Did you know she raised a
glass of Vichy water, said "Here's to love"
and died?
It should have been champagne.
Too many babies, her life
all sour milk, nappies, compromises.
Dear love, do not waste your strength in
weeping.
Rejoice in me instead.
When we go to Rome I will take great care of
you,
I will wear red.

1907

Will you come on Satyrday
Or shall it be the atelier
Where all the world must go away
So I can have my kisses?
When I was hardly more than a little girl
I used to think how I would love someone.
I would put my arms around him
and not let go
until he understood
standing there
all that I said in silence
my body and my heart eloquent
beyond all words –
then
naturally
he would love me.

It was always you.

I washed my velvet jacket
it has faded to a dark rose
I think you looked at it last time
it is lovelier now, so soft.
Notice, tomorrow, in the candle light.

1907

Aloneness is near God
        but can I bear it?
I have borne insult and neglect

When I'm honest you say it's unbecoming
in a woman
as if desire were something pitiable

I made a dress after a Manet painting
but when I wore it my father called me whore.

Whistler told me
        painting is a matter of marks, of glazes
                and of tone,
things subtle and precise
accomplished in solitude
out of long looking
        finding the form

I do it well by now.
It's not enough.

I can suffer in my flesh but not deny it
without it my soul wanders

like the old woman in the market:
she has forgotten the names of fruit
tiny eyes squinting: *"C'est bien une poire,
mademoiselle?"*
"Mais non madame, ce sont des pommes", very firm
am I.
She weighs one in each hand, doubtfully.
Apple? *Apple? Pear.*

I watch you during Mass at Notre-Dame.
Communion, the high altar.
When I lift my breasts before you in the light
what are you but my communicant?
As I am yours. Reply.

1907

Arched in an arabesque
my *corps admirable*
becomes a tree an amphora
hauled briny from the sea
still breathing fumes of wine.

I watch you watching me
never the paper
never your own hand.
The *Muse* is armless
how can she hold you?
How indeed can I?
You have no time for us
oh but you find time for the other one:
her dead red wig bobs between your knees;
I call her coarse murderess
and am cast out of Heaven for my hate
while you swagger in new suits,
a foolish peasant boy
who used to be a god.

I am your truest wife
I am the one. Deep-rooted dark blue flower,
I bloom in darkness there outside the gate.

1908

This morning as you left
you turned back at the door and smiled
and then you put your finger on your lips
like that tiny Roman bronze in the Louvre:
"Harpocrates, god of silence."

How silly!
Without my letters I might as well be mute.
To whom would I speak, shy as I am?
Madame Rodin, or your scary amie?
No: to you, only to you.
Trust me.

Dear love, I blew a kiss
but you were gone.

1908

MELISANDE: Non, non, restons ici...Je suis plus près de toi dans l'obscurité....
 – Maeterlinck, Pelléas et Melisande, act four

I take the little train from Montparnasse
to Meudon-Val Fleury or to Petit-Clamart,
marching straight on as though I know
exactly where I'm bound.
By now, of course, I do:
the park, the long alley of elms that leads
to your white gate.
I watch the window: will your shadow pass,
loom godlike up before the yellow lamp?
Moonscumbled clouds float open, like a flower –
so would I be for you, my first last only love.
– Voices. I dart back to darkest trees.
Substantial men tramp forth, I wait, I follow;
with my big coat and my umbrella I am shapeless,
invisible, spent, a clumsy bird with frozen feet.
Why do I do this?
The rattling train, the long walk out through snow,
my fear of louche encounters in the dark;
and, should we meet, I know how cross you'd

be –
the lion's blazing rage, the gazelle dead with fright –

Here, feel my runaway heart.
I write you from my room, to say good night.

1908

Oh mon petit chat
Sauvage dans les bois
As-tu donc oublié
Ta vie d'autrefois?
  – Gwen John

I am Miss Edgar-Quinet,
why would I forget a thing?
Distractions, though, occur:
Ants on a stem of grass, dog-piss, thirst.
Of course I've heard you call me from the grove,
Seen you beweep my absence as you've wept for his.
Some nights I purr – so near you!
It is perfect love.
That torment of song is the doomed nightingale.
You'd snatch it free (crunch crunch), I know.
This time I won't come home. You've failed.
I am pure Calicat, black-orange blazoned queen
of thickets, with white paws and tail.
You named me for a street, now let me roam.
Sometimes I'm flat with fear: a dog howls,
or the hawk sinks silent down. No hiding place in frost
Or drenching rain. I watch your moonlit sleep.

Your palm unclenches, tastes of salt.
I shiver in my fur. We both are lost now. Lost.

1909

Your promises unkept
have hurt my heart.
Plums, bonbons (I unwrapped each one
carefully, smoothing the thin paper
that whispered in my hand
colored like petals or like things that fly)
yes and silk roses, too.
I blow the dust away.

I've settled for a little trumpery trash,
"fine knacks for ladies," (do you know that
English song?)
"A beggar may be liberal of love."
Well, you made me a mendicant
when I craved but to give you
all that quivers in my mind
as in my secret parts;
all that in me divine
and my own quiet art.

1910

But for Rodin the woman . . . is like nourishment for the man, like a drink which courses through him ever and anon: like wine. He believes in wine.
– Rainer Maria Rilke, letter to Clara Rilke, September 1908

There, almost at my feet, bobbing in the Seine,
all white and swollen, glazed with opal light.
Oh maître, think how lonely,
how desperate she must have been to die like that!
How frightful to be without hope, and know it.
They dragged her out with long hooked
poles, her dark dress
shapeless, brown water poured out of it, yes,
and a fish, too,
writhing astonished
till one man in pity grabbed it, cast it back
with a flat sound on the river.
The weight of water made her dress so still,
carved folds and ridges in the (I now see) dark green wool:
in your studio you have a block of stone that color,
from a quarry in the Appenines, you said.

Your laughter in the firelight –
you said I was your vin nouveau,
fresh, new, bright on the tongue.
I quenched your thirst,
then you awakened mine.
Five years ago, mon maître.

I think I won't go on the river again,
not till summer.
She must have died of sorrow, n'est-ce-pas?
For no one dies of love, only for want of it.
I went into a bar and drank hot spiced wine,
wanting that heat all through me.
I believe in wine.

1912

I lay in bed all night thinking of you
hearing the coal man's cat
coughing
down in the courtyard
until the paler window told me
I must sleep
or be pale myself today
when I pose for English virgins
of a certain age:
Miss Bowser
Miss Leigh
Miss Lloyd
Miss Hart who hates men
Miss O'Donel who hates me.

When I slept felt your thigh
press against mine
it was so real
and then I dreamed you kissed me
delicately
between my breasts
as once you did.

1914

The street trembles,
basements, other people's prayers –
I am saner if not safer in my room.
You sent a hundred francs.
How dear mon maître that you think of me
amid the confusion of war
the fearsome noise and sorrow
so that my heart blooms: poppy in a golden field

> heavily you bend to pluck it
> blowing just out of reach
> crumpled red silk
> a dress you said you liked.

1917

I was not there at your cold end.
The heating system died, and then Madame,
then you. Not even a last scrawl.
If they had let me in
I would have kept you warm,
wrapped in my long limbs and my cashmere
shawl.

When I try to pray, names of colours come
instead:
alizarin crimson, vermilion, rouge outremer,
hot outposts of the Orient –
or phrases like
"exquisite brazen clamour of odalisques"
signifying – what?

I cannot sleep
not knowing what you want.

1917

Rilke, help me.
How can I come to rest?

At Swansea long ago after a storm
I saw a great tree shrug off
its ruined limbs and crown,
then, all that summer, die.

Where is he now?
If I lie down
and will myself to stone
might I come near him?
Does music hear me, bear me,
birdsong behind bruised lips?

No angel speaks to me,
Blackness thickens,
yawns between the stars.

I'm frightened.   Take my hand.

1919

They keep hay in it.
It is not fine or grand.
I think I shall be alone there.
I could work.

I may have found the Beast's enchanted house
just outside Pléneuf, in Brittany.
Clematis tangle, green blur through wavy glass,
a towering tile stove all swagged cerulean blue.
This place is called le Manoir de Vauxclair
which means clear valley or valley of light.
The air is limpid here,
where fritillaries ride it down to beckoning
weeds.
Cats came at once to greet me.
A high round room. Fresh eggs.

1926

Chère Mademoiselle Véra,
Thank you for saying God doesn't mind if I
draw in church.
I do it reverently.

I stay beside myself.
I wait.
How will I know
it's faith?

> *I love you as I love white flowers.*
> *You are soft and kind.*

My cats dance in the leaves.
To think of God as "father"
hurts my mind.
Teach me to pray for Rilke
killed by a rose.

Until Monday, then.

Amitiés,

    Gwen John

1927

Chère Mademoiselle,

I cannot meet your eyes
(those long long eyes).
You would feel compassion
would you not
for some little animal you'd saved from death?

Well, you saved me from death.
You should feel tenderness for me,
a little animal scrabbling in the dark.
I cannot live as other people do.

I know that those in Purgatory
suffer as I do now.
How can you say my letters to you
are bad for my soul?
They *are* my soul.

Every Monday when I come to tea
I will bring you a drawing:
les dessins de lundi.
These are the only prayers I know by heart.

1930   pour Mlle Véra

Delayed dismayed mislaid.
Twilight. *Crépuscule.*
Black leaves on streaks of sky.
A last least band of blue.
Dry pigment stained in squares.
The linen shows.
Worn down to stubble my good sable brush.
As. For. Subject.

A man a cat it's the same thing.

Eloquence? I can't.
Words shatter on the air.
To speak in shards is shame.
I write it out. Bits set down with care.
Recopied. And again. Again.

Cedilla, circumflex, grave and aigu.
My screed all marred with hairball and with tea.
I try: a little cough, a sigh.
You never look at me.
What good my being good?
You still won't look.
– Here is my view outside before new buildings

rise.
Few strokes on a warped board,
Davy's grey, green earth, jaune de Naples
rougeâtre.
To say "Naples yellow, reddish" – not the same,
just as "roadside" or "verge" is not at all
"le bord de la route".
It is that color, there.

I am not holy. I often long for lies.
So late. Light drains to midnight.
This this oh only this is true:
I could come close to God
if I were close to you.

1930

To defend ourselves from the invasions of our neighbours, we are going to try and see if it is possible to live at Meudon without losing all leisure for prayer, and without endangering our very lives.
        — Jacques Maritain

I saw the Gate of Hell
for six years, every day,
aswarm with human torment
fixed in bronze.
I never dreamed
a note pinned on a door
would cast me to the damned.
On the tympanum at Conques
carved Satan flogs his creatures into Hell
with his great long member;
but you let fall those words from your thin mouth.
Chapeau for such economy of means.

"Mad boundless love of God," you droned,
l'amour fou et sans bornes
yet now you have fixed a boundary
I may not cross. I freeze, I burn.
I am a naked child in a bleak field

no shelter here but stones
or that dark cloud I dread.
When I become a little heap of bones
I think that God will scold you
for not loving me enough, alive or dead.

1932

Now all my things have left the rue Terre Neuve
for this walled garden full of cats and weeds.
My shack in rue Babié quakes in the breeze,
some lacustrine ancestress on stilt stubby legs;
a slow girl who sees her own reflection when it rains,
and only then
she takes me in.

It is so lovely I forget to eat.

nearer to God
nearer to nature which *is* God after all
although M. le curé disputes this as I suppose he must,
busy as he is with human life, birth to dust.
Some say I seek belief because I'm going mad.
Or, that I'm crazed for wanting to believe
I can make my steep way to sainthood, starved and unkempt,
hands bloodied on the crags.

Forgive my sins and the time wasted

(Yet I read that Marie-Magdalène
after thirty years of meditation and humility in Provence
washed her hands in a spring that miraculously appeared in her cave,
cried 'Oh les belles mains!' and had to stay dirty for another thirty years.

"Mad as a lemon squeezer," sweet Ida called herself,
boxed in by babies till she fled to death.
I have not those distractions (or distinctions) yet.

I do have my lakeless lake-dwelling in rue Babié,
my striped strays in the garden they enchant.
Don't think (as before) to work for years ahead.
You work for one moment. Paint. Pain. Pray.

1933

Which region shall I wander in?
    The land of flowers.
Ursula, you asked about the watercolours at Lefranc,
I can tell you the exact tones.

Cinabre clair is the colour of the little ball holding the snowdrop petals.
Rouge phénicien, the stem of the wild geranium.
Laque de Smyrne foncé, the tufted roses now in flower.
And, Vert anglais is those green tubs in front of your hotel.

Thank you for sending the perfect coat and skirt.
I shall be élégante and warm sometimes.
For the rest, I try to paint for God.
Gouache or ink on paper now,
the same thing a hundred times repeated,
trying to find perfection.
Surely the place where it exists
that parabola
between my hand and nature
is not this world.

1936

Blue shawl crumpled on the chair's pale arm,
a furled umbrella,
another limp dark dress.
The ceiling is a slant of yellow light.

My nearest likeness is an empty room
that God must fill.
These days I cast no shadow
drawn as I am to things ineffable but hard
as minerals: soul, spirit, Heaven, Hell.

Each day divides itself from bell to holy bell.
I meditate, I read saints' lives,
I pray to Rilke, to Prince Myshkin as well,
sit quietly in church; I draw housewives,
children, nuns. No one minds.
But if I cry out, then who will answer me?
Mild Jesus, or Saint Michael? Joan of Arc?
– That dazzling light off armour hurts my eyes.
Sainte Thérèse, *ma presque contemporaine*,
Please be my sister. I will not paint again.
Accept this sacrifice.

.

1939

Je vous salue Marie —
    he called me that,
    "Gwen" impossible in French;
    he did try GVENNG? *GVENNE?* but declined
    to be ridiculous.
So I became Marie
for after all he was Julie for a time,
Julie, my little confidante
to whom I spoke my heart: *I'm sewing a blue*
dress. Do you think my lover will like it?
Renuncio.

The Feast of the Assumption he said was my
own fête
la fête de Marie
        John Mary, Mary Jones, I am all of them,
                blest and *blessée*
 among women (his face over mine, smiling; my
own blood)

Pain after all is most of *paint.*
It twists inside me now
Je suis habitée de douleur
and so   *renuncio*

Love of Rodin, love of Véra, love of God:
the same shut door
I knelt to as the altar of a saint.

Hurry   the northbound train   I'll travel light
as light   *renuncio*

At Dieppe I will dissolve into sea air
No one will find my body anywhere.

September 18, 1939

The priest has come to annoy anoint me
(his foolish pockmarked face! Enfin
I gasp out "Bless me father" to someone who
looks fourteen)
oh well the holy words the sacraments
must bear me out of life, the speaker matters not

    I had supposed a great billowing wave,
not this opaque weight
    a brutish lover forcing down

light fades
to none at all
    only heaviness
    Da's parlour drapes drawn plush stained
    salt and semen
    the slap of the sea outside unseen
    stuffed birds rise from glass dooms
    creak their dead wings
    dark in the room's own dark

I try to say Credo
CREDO
    shale and surf in my throat

Oh mon Maître je regrette toute chose mal exprimée
c'est que finalement je suis faible

> Ida's star in the water glass
> blooms to twin sparks: my lost cat's eyes!

I burst into eternal love
clasping soft fur.

1961: GUS

"In fifty years I shall be remembered only as her brother."
— Augustus John

Fame and lust outlived by me,
Stumbling in sad parody
Of what once I aspired to be:
Modest, true, and blest as she.

Sister, lost in opal skies,
Safe from love and all its lies,
Unlike me, too chaste, too wise –
See.

God and cats and saints and paint,
All these – life's company – renounced,
Soeur et complice, you've slipped away
To quiet death, all unannounced.
Oblivion. A pauper's grave. I carry on, but why?

Me.

Gypsies still hail me, tease grave bows from a bear,
An ape salutes, ashimmer in green silk.
Tumult of women and brave-painted carts.

Tears blind me when they smile and call me "Rai."
Who knows that now? No harm. Less art.
Whose spotted hands are these?
Young daughters warm my bed but will not stay.
Old mumper's mutterings, my lass, my rover,
Where have you gone, my featherbreast, my plover,
That you turn not to me in your soft hair?
I am your brother.
I make haste, I listen, I wait.
I query every mist. Oh where?

Here.

MOVING OUT

TEN JAPONAISERIES

1. Silence is movement.
   Kimono following sword:
   Moments in a dance.

2. Miyagawa painted me
   barefoot in snowfall
   in a silver robe.

3. I *am* the Floating World –
   rumor of silk on bristle;
   fishheads too, and rouge.

4. Monochrome in moonlight,
   dearest ghost, wide-eyed,
   haunt me to tearless sleep.

5. Lamp. Clock.
   Chrysanthemums (long life).
   Perhaps the dawn could come much later?

6. At sundown, Mother,
   returning from the baths,
   you warned me of men's wiles.

7. I pose to please you, Hiroshige,
   Just a hint of red silk
   Showing.

8. The threads of autumn yield
   jitter and scroop of silk.
   Never too busy for love.

9. Blotting the lipstick –
   What's left? A jewel, a scarab
   if scarabs came blood-red.

10. Brutally, from behind.
    My face tells nothing.
    Only an indrawn breath.

VA

Sun on the ridge but blurred
because the pines breathe blue:
des exhalations résineuses.
Overwhelmingly
(if I close my eyes)
Provence
(I don't, I
won't).

IN

Dogwood and redbud again!
Morels!
I
stayed away so long
there's
no way back.

TX

Rattlers, coyotes, big buzzards.
Keep that cat inside.
A girl in tooled turquoise boots
kicks at the dirt, tastes it,
lifts her ecstatic face
to the sweet first rain.

NH

Black ice –
short flight to the guardrail
then a big drift
180º around.
People here are kind.
They give you tea
and an 800 number
when you land stunned
in their curve.

OR

"A particularly subtle and delicate
grey-green paint on the better buildings"
(a metaphor for damp?)
ORegon, ORpheus, rain swells
the river of souls
clinging fiercely to Willamette's edge
borne unready to the sea
singing.

CA

Lupines and poppies,
fire in the hills.
First smell of the sea,
first glimpse of it
through a taut pink hat
in my grandmother's geranium lap.

PG

– Little towns that war and earthquakes marred.
Polychrome angels hoist fat candles
while we pray for the three drunken brothers:
for Mario ('his father was a drunkard and his mother
a keg of wine'); for Nanni who made love to a cow;
for Beppe whose dog was cleverer than he.
All, all wafted to heaven
on the smoke of black *Toscanelli* cigars.
Some nights I'd hear them cry out through the wall
in wonder or in pain, *'Porca madonna!'*
Choked coughing. Clink of jug on glass.
Lady of Mercies, even angels fall.
Here, Queen of Heaven, three pure courtiers come.

CH

Don't believe what they say:
love dies with the lover,
burns up, rots in earth.
      (Shy pilgrimage to azaleas
        you have these twelve years fed)

Le plein, s'il vous plaît, fill the tank,
who knew I still could cry? –
in a Swiss gas station
whose owner also mans
le four crématoire.

VT

The Snow Cat
for Sydney Lea

Now new snow blurs the tracks
I've barely read:
Squirrel and deer; the alko lady's
polydactyl cat, each print a seven-petaled
flower.
By the first poplars they're all going. Gone.

Kneedeep in anything is shit.
Turn back. It's time.
The scraps of fur and bone
I saw last spring
are scattered deep by now,
are not

at all.

I plunge back up the hill,
no good at country, winter, death;
knowing the bears are right:
curl silently to sleep,
wear a white wreath of breath.

In my throat
the dead cat
spreads her claws.

AZ

for Fox and Bruce McGrew

Nothing more different than this, than here:
Five months of snow and dark.

That week at Oracle the sunlight showered
down like rain.
Each night the moon bobbed with us in the pool.
Dazzled, it seemed so right that we should stay
– part of your light, my dears –
but deaths and houses sent us far away.

Once, in the mail, your picture, filled with
worlds.
It helps.

So sick of maple syrup, cheddar, hyperborean
cheer.
Please write. Send chiles and pine nuts soon.
We dream of you. We'll come another year.

NM: ROSWELL
for Don and Sally Anderson

"Eschewing the merely picturesque"
the flat high desert
gets you anyway.

One distant cone of mountain;
another one, with snow. El Capitán,
Sierra Blanca.

One strip mall. Various UFO's,
Ristras. Honey, the scene is set,
all right? Tonight let's eat at Sonic,
get the feel of time suspended, oh,
about 1958. We are just three years wed.

Upon dull tan adobes and the parched blond
grass
the sunset sky heartbreakingly bestows
festoons of lemon, indigo, an apricot's ripe
heart.
Low riders prowl Berrenedo, lights winking red.

MEDITERRANEO

– the sea in the middle of the world
        amphoras alphabets alabasters
anchovies artifacts bronze amorini and athletes
all these come to shore alla riva marina
        riding small waves

far out the fisherman lets down his lines
        feels the weight of a vase
        depicting a blue feline face
        of great beauty, sacred to Isis
stella maris protectress of crops and of vessels
puissant goddess return me to my self once more

        What do the shards say?
Lost encipherings, inventories, checklists,
                prayers and scandals:
Domitilla likes it or *Faustus stultus est*

We keep prowling flea markets:
        Arezzo, Porta Portese, silted-up Rimini
of lace-crusted linens and fierce Nigerian
whores,
always just missing
   something desirable: no time and less money.

Have no regrets.
Had you bought it
it would have fled you like quicksilver.
At least you have glimpsed us
in a fragmented tile
or silvery votive.
It's the eyes that insist
(peering out through laurel
or waterfall):
We are waiting.
We are the world's end
Do not think you can reach us.

FROM A NEUTRAL COUNTRY

For days and days I kept on writing you
from a neutral country; an urgent letter,
precise and present as a Swatch,
spelling it out, wanting to make sure
you understood.
       I tore it up.

Too many words to tell you
what I hope you know –
I loved you irreparably.
Regrets? Beaucoup. Toujours.

Now, perpend:
75 years ago, in another canton,
Rilke sighs adieux
to Balthus' raging mother.
Her soft breasts: his starch.
Noli me tangere. Her tears.
Peonies flung down, bruised against rainy tiles.
Things broken. Keepsakes gone.
Our citrus-scented nights.
A knowing child.

And so it somehow is

that a girl with a cat swoons back in dusty light
forever, watched by a fierce
dwarf.

Should you in autumn enter
rooms like these, where yearning chokes the air,
remember me: I am the manatee,
out of her depth and yours,
offering a kiss.

KNOSSOS
In memory of Raimonda Buitoni

She was an Athenian girl,
my mother,
shipped here as tribute or as sacrifice
(much the same).
A dancer, she was agile, she survived.
Learning the labyrinth, at the end
she never had to touch the fraying thread
      some woman left behind.
Unseen, she slipped into the light,
bore me amid a field of cyclamens,
      and died.

Strangers undid me from her stiffening
breast,
cleaned me and fed me, harbored me as
theirs.
They feared that gods lurked somewhere in
my line –
newborn, I came with whorls of wheaten hair,
prinked out with buds of wild anemone.

Those good folk tried to warn me:
"Now dear, if some bull, or swan, or spotted

Pard . . .!"
I heard, I sighed. At last I murmured,
"What can I do if some immortal god
pretends to be my pet, and pounces, purring?
Claws in, paws kneading my taut breasts,
he IS my own big cat."

Too late. The ichor's in my veins.
The new moon's shaped like my true father's
head.
Feed me ambrosia, then, or roasted swine.
I'm more (and less) than human.
Tireless, locusts shrill.
Were they once someone else?
I spill a new libation: dark red wine.

THE PUZZLEMISTRESS
for Judith Bagai

At fifteen she was all sonnets and effluvia –
Blood, sperm, homunculi.
She grew up, fled. Puns, ciphers, palindromes
in their great purity
drew near and sheltered her.
In the round tower she shook out her hair,
transmuted DOOM to MOOD,
the demon MODO morphed to DOMO, scuttled home.
When synapses died and blurred her lovely brain
The sighing river crested at A NIP,
Caressed her with I NAP, transforming PAIN.

Oh you who haunt the riverbank, breasting dark air,
Remember Judith, who once was quick and fair.

FLO

Oh tell me quick and give me joy
That I may find my sweet sailor boy

Quicksilver sister,
Daughter whose laughter persists past all loss,
Sailor lad, castaway: all dance in a downpour
where the storm ferries houses through treetops
while you dream of whitecaps and striped
jerseys.

"There's not much sexier than a man who knits,"
you mused, purling two. A last kiss.

Let's go on out, break a few hearts.
It's still early. Light takes flight.
Set sail for an island
that smells now of death and of vetiver,
broken place where my child
fed on night.

THE UNFORTUNATE LADY

She was never the same after Etna erupted
and lava came roiling through the blood-orange grove,
scorching the shutters she pulled tightly shut,
gasping, hand on heart, packing, fleeing back home.

In Vermont she shakes her head, moans
"Taormina," and sighs.

She was never herself once her head hit the pavement
and a pool of peach ice-cream;
but she staggered up, addled, declining all help.
Not the same, not the same, not ever the same.

I will go to an island. I will live like Gauguin.

Guavas and mangoes. A stretch in the sun.
My skin's brown as yours now. You must love me forever.

A green sky. She shudders. All the insects are still.

The tsunami gathers, embracing all waters
from the thick and unthinkable deeps of the sea.
So is she. So does she.

www.ingramcontent.com/pod-product-compliance
Lightning Source LLC
Chambersburg PA
CBHW031301290426
44109CB00012B/671